# devotionals from famous hymn stories

## lindsay l. terry

**BAKER BOOK HOUSE**
Grand Rapids, Michigan 49506

To
**TENNESSEE TEMPLE SCHOOLS**

Chattanooga, Tennessee

where I first learned to love
the study of hymnology

## ACKNOWLEDGMENTS

I would like to express my appreciation to my wife, Marilyn, for many hours spent typing the manuscript, and to Dr. Lee Roberson, pastor of the Highland Park Baptist Church, Chattanooga, Tennessee, for writing the introduction.

Much valuable information was gained from such books as Ira Sankey's *My Life and Story of the Gospel Hymns, Lyric Religion, The Story of My Ninety-four Years,* by S. Trevena Jackson, *Music in Evangelism,* by Phil Kerr, and many, many others.

Stories were received directly from such noted authors and composers as Mr. Mosie Lister, Mr. Virgil P. Brock, Dr. Oswald J. Smith and Mrs. Lois Johnson Fritsch. Mrs. H. A. Dye sent interesting information concerning Mr. C. Austin Miles, composer of "In the Garden."

# CONTENTS

## PREFACE

Each devotional in this book is appropriate as an opening devotional for any Christian group. Everyone likes a good story, especially one that is filled with emotion and human interest. Such are these stories. Some contain elements of adventure; others, character sketches; some are related to major historical events. All are true stories about real people involved in real circumstances, out of which grew some of our best loved hymns.

These devotionals are based on my research, interviews, and correspondence. Some are presented the first time, almost exactly as I received them from the composers. Stories were received directly from such noted authors and composers as Mr. Mosie Lister, Mr. Virgil P. Brock, Dr. Oswald J. Smith, and Mrs. Lois Johnson Fritsch. Mrs. H. A. Dye sent interesting information concerning Mr. C. Austin Miles, composer of "In the Garden."

I would like to express my appreciation to my wife, Marilyn, for many hours spent typing the manuscript.

May these devotionals enrich your appreciation for our great heritage of hymns and gospel songs.

Lindsay Terry

# INTRODUCTION

No one can estimate the full value of music in the work of the Lord! Down through the centuries songs have been pouring out of the hearts of men and women—songs which tell us of God's love, His grace, His mercy, and His dealings with the hearts of men. My own heart rejoices in the way that God has used so many to give to the world songs that bless and inspire.

Lindsay Terry has done a good work in presenting these *Family Devotionals from Famous Hymn Stories.* His stories about songs increase our love for the songs of Zion. Mr. Terry is an excellent musician, but above all he is a Christian. His heart is in tune with God and his love for music reflects his devotion to the Savior. It is a joy for me to commend this book. Read it, rejoice in it!

Lee Roberson
Chattanooga, Tennessee

# 1

## WE NEED A PILOT

**SCRIPTURE: Mark 4:30-41**

*And he arose and rebuked the wind, and said unto the sea, Peace, be still. And the wind ceased, and there was a great calm.*

Many of the great songs of the church compare the path of life to a great voyage on the sea.

Edward Hopper was born in New York City in 1818. Mr. Hopper was a very humble man, refusing credit for his contributions in the field of hymn-writing. He rarely signed his name to his work, and in the cases where he did, he often used a pen name.

After graduation from the Union Theological Seminary in 1832, he held pastorates in Greenville, New York, and Sag Harbor, Long Island. From the Sag Harbor church he returned to his hometown and became pastor of the Church of the Sea and Land which he served until his death in 1888. During this last pastorate the kindly old gentleman was busy tending the needs of the men who sailed the seven seas. He wrote songs for them to sing in the services and on their journeys.

How happy is the man who can give himself in service to others. It is said of General William Booth, founder of the Salvation Army, that in his latter years failing health kept him from attending one of the annual conventions. Yet he sent a message to be read to the convention. It simply said:

"OTHERS!" That's what serving Christ is all about: knowing Him and then sharing Him with others.

The song that made Hopper so famous was sung for nine years before he was known as the author.

> Jesus, Savior, pilot me
> Over life's tempestuous sea;
> Unknown waves before me roll,
> Hiding rocks and treacherous shoal;
> Chart and compass come from Thee:
> Jesus, Savior, pilot me.
>
> As a mother stills her child,
> Thou canst hush the ocean wild;
> Boisterous waves obey Thy will
> When Thou sayest to them, "Be still!"
> Wondrous Sovereign of the sea,
> Jesus, Savior, pilot me.

**REFLECTION:** You, if you are a Christian, serve the God who controls the seas, with their ebb and flow, their dashing, tossing waves. Surely He can also calm the tempest in your soul when you feel so helpless. He cares and He wants to be your pilot. Turn the wheel over to Him!

# 2

## JOY AT CHRISTMAS TIME

**SCRIPTURE: Matthew 1:18–2:12**

*When they saw the star, they rejoiced with exceeding great joy.*

One of our most popular Christmas carols is the result of the efforts of two truly great men: Isaac Watts and George Frederick Handel. Handel, a large, robust, outspoken man, was quite different from Watts who was a frail, sickly, quiet man only five feet tall. Both men lived in London. They were acquainted and each must have appreciated the other's talents.

In 1719, Isaac Watts, already a notable hymn writer, sat down under a tree at the Abney Estate near London and began to write some verses based on Psalm 98. Little did he realize the popularity and fame that his verses would receive.

In 1741 George Frederick Handel, who was already famous as the composer of several operas and oratorios, decided that he wanted to do a truly great work. After spending some time in prayer, he arose from his knees and for twenty-three days labored almost continuously day and night. The immortal *Messiah* was the fruit of that incessant labor. From this masterpiece, which for more than two centuries has been heralded as one of the greatest of sacred classics, has come the basis for many other compositions.

A nobleman once praised Handel for the entertainment he had furnished in the music of "He Was Despised and Rejected." In no uncertain terms Handel let the nobleman know that his music was composed to make men better, not to entertain them.

Almost a hundred years later, Boston's choir-director-composer, Lowell Mason, adapted a portion of *Messiah* to fit the poem Isaac Watts had written in 1719. In every Christmas season we hear around the world, the resounding strains of: (Don't read it, sing it!)

Joy to the world! the Lord is come.
Let earth receive her King;
Let every heart prepare Him room,
And heaven and nature sing,
And heaven and nature sing,
And heaven, and heaven and nature sing.

Joy to the earth! the Savior reigns.
Let men their songs employ,
While fields and floods, rocks, hills, and plains
Repeat the sounding joy,
Repeat the sounding joy,
Repeat, repeat the sounding joy.

**REFLECTION**: In every corner of the globe where men have carried the message of Christ, there has been joy. Christ sets the captive free and puts a song in hearts. He redeems souls. He reigns as King in the hearts of men. He lifts the status of women from slavery to wife and mother. He causes men to clean up their bodies as well as their lives. And He can bring joy to you if you really hear the message, "Joy to the world! the Lord is come."

# 3

## ASSURANCE

**SCRIPTURE: Isaiah 48:10-22**

*O that thou hadst hearkened to my commandments! then had thy peace been as a river, and thy righteousness as the waves of the sea.*

There is a most tragic story behind the writing of the hymn "It Is Well with my Soul."

H. G. Spafford was a successful businessman of Chicago with a lovely family of six—a wife and five children. On November 21, 1873, the French liner, *Ville du Havre* was crossing the Atlantic from America to France. On board were Mrs. Spafford and four of the children. Suddenly, the steamer collided with a large sailing vessel. As the panic started, Mrs. Spafford hurriedly brought the four children to the deck. She knelt there with them in prayer, asking God to spare them if it could be His will, or to make them willing to die if that was His will.

Within two hours the ship slipped beneath the dark waters of the Atlantic, carrying with it most of its passengers, including the four Spafford children. A sailor was rowing over the spot where the ship had sunk when he spotted a woman floating in the water. It was Mrs. Spafford. Nine days later she landed safely in Cardiff, Wales. From there she sent her husband this message: "Saved Alone." Mr. Spafford framed this telegram and hung it in his office.

Mr. Spafford booked passage on the first available ship and left to join his heartbroken wife. One night the captain told him, "I believe we are now passing over the spot where the *Ville du Havre* went down. Mr. Spafford could not sleep. He began to write " . . . when sorrows like sea billows roll . . . whatever my lot . . . it is well with my soul."

When peace, like a river, attendeth my way,
When sorrows like sea billows roll;
Whatever my lot, Thou hast taught me to say,
It is well, it is well with my soul.

And, Lord, haste the day when the faith shall be sight,
The clouds be rolled back as a scroll,
The trump shall resound and the Lord shall descend;
Even so—it is well with my soul.

Chorus:
It is well with my soul,
It is well, it is well with my soul.

**REFLECTION**: God will give us His peace when we meet His requirements. Many times He sends unusual circumstances into our lives to make us more like His Son. If all things are accepted as from Him, then His peace is the result.

# 4

## THE CHILDREN LOVE THE BACHELOR

### SCRIPTURE: Matthew 2:1-15

*And thou Bethlehem, in the land of Juda, art not the least among the princes of Juda: for out of thee shall come a Governor, that shall rule my people Israel.*

"O Mother, how happy the angels will be!" was the startling and yet tender comment of a child who was a member of the church of which Phillips Brooks was pastor when she heard of his passing on to heaven.

There is an old adage: "His hat may be greasy and his trousers may not be creased, but if his children flatten their noses against the windowpane thirty minutes before he comes home from work, you can trust him with anything you have." Phillips Brooks had no children of his own: in fact, he was never married, but he loved the children of his congregations very dearly, and they returned the affection.

It was under his ministry that the Holy Trinity Church of Boston became such a renowned lighthouse. He preached, unlike most Protestants of his day in that city, the evangelical gospel of Jesus Christ. He was six and a half feet tall and, from all I can gather, he must have possessed the kindness of a Washington, the poise of a Lincoln, the fire of a Sunday, and the delivery of a Bryan.

In 1865, he was granted a leave of absence from his church in Philadelphia to visit the Holy Land. He visited the place of the shepherds and joined in the traditional services on Christmas eve at The Church of the Nativity. This was such a memorable experience for him that he later wrote a poem for the children of his Sunday school.

The next day he gave the poem to Lewis Redner who was the organist and Sunday school superintendent, and asked him to set it to music. On Saturday, the night before Christmas, Redner still had not come up with the music. During the night he awakened with a new tune ringing in his ears. He quickly jotted down the notes and promptly went back to sleep. He arose early the next morning and wrote the harmony for the new song in time for the children to sing it at Sunday school.

The carol remained relatively unknown for about twenty years, and then it was published in an Episcopal hymnal. From that time its popularity has spread until now at Christmas time people everywhere sing:

> O little town of Bethlehem,
> How still we see thee lie!
> Above thy deep and dreamless sleep
> The silent stars go by;
> Yet in thy dark streets shineth
> The everlasting Light:
> The hopes and fears of all the years
> Are met in thee tonight.

**REFLECTION**: Of course we can see why the children loved Phillips Brooks. He loved them and took time out from his busy schedule to make sure that the children shared in one of the most memorable occasions of his lifetime. Not only did he share this occasion with them, but with us also. We still enjoy his unselfishness.

# 5

## OUT OF DARKNESS, A SUNBEAM

**SCRIPTURE: Romans 8:26-39**

*Nay, in all these things we are more than conquerors through him that loved us.*

The story behind this hymn is remarkably similar to that behind the hymn, "No One Ever Cared for Me Like Jesus." Both were born out of dark sorrow.

Dr. George Matheson was another of the great preachers produced by Scotland. He was born there in 1842. While still in his teens, he entered the University of Glasgow. He was stricken with total blindness shortly after his entrance into school. But not even the loss of eyesight could stop George Matheson.

Before his death, Mr. Matheson recorded his own account of the writing of his masterpiece, "O Love That Wilt Not Let Me Go." The hymn was composed in the manse of Innellan on the evening of June 6, 1882. He was alone in the manse. It was the day of his sister's marriage, and the rest of the family were staying overnight in Glasgow. Some event, known only to him, caused him the most severe mental suffering. It has been suggested that he was in love with a young lady and was jilted. This may have been the reason for his extreme distress. The hymn was a fruit of that suffering.

He reported that the hymn was the quickest bit of work he ever did in his life. It seemed to be dictated to him by some inward voice. The whole work was completed in five minutes and it never received any retouching or correction.

> O love that wilt not let me go,
> I rest my weary soul in Thee;

I give Thee back the life I owe,
That in Thine ocean depths its flow
May richer, fuller be.

**REFLECTION:** It is only the tremendous love that God has for us that causes Him to draw a curtain over our future so that we cannot see what lies ahead. Therefore, we must cling to Him for daily strength and daily guidance. Truly this makes our lives richer and fuller.

# 6

## UNMERITED FAVOR

**SCRIPTURE**: Ephesians 2:1-18

*For by grace are ye saved through faith; and that not of yourselves: it is the gift of God: Not of works, lest any man should boast.*

"John Newton, Clerk, once an infidel and libertine, a servant of slaves in Africa, was by the rich mercy of our Lord and Saviour, Jesus Christ preserved, restored, pardoned, and appointed to preach the faith he had long labored to destroy near sixteen years at Olney in Bucks and . . . years in this Church . . . "

The above is the epitaph, written by his own hand, of a man who has made more than a small contribution to the singing of happy Christians. His deeply religious mother, at whose knee he learned many a Bible text, passed away when he was only seven. After just two years of schooling he went to sea with his father, a skipper, and for eighteen years sailed the seven seas.

Newton spent six of these wanton years as captain of a slave ship which landed some of its human freight in Charleston, South Carolina. The young Newton grew into a wild, profligate, and blasphemous sailor.

On a long voyage from Brazil the young sailor fell to reading *Imitation of Christ,* by Thomas á Kempis. Later, during a vicious storm that threatened to send his ship to the bottom of the sea, he began to think of the Christ about whom he had read in the book. He was soon converted and became an ardent student of the Bible.

He resigned as a sailor in 1748, but not one person in England would have guessed that Captain John Newton was leaving the sea to preach the gospel. He studied for sixteen long years and was finally ordained and sent to be the pastor of a small church in Olney.

When at eighty years of age he was urged by his friends to give up his preaching because he was no longer able to read his text, he replied, "What! Shall the old African blasphemer stop while he can speak?" This was typical of the fighting spirit that characterized his useful life.

In his last days, Captain John Newton walked to the pulpit of one of England's greatest churches, dressed as a sailor, and preached the unsearchable riches of the grace of God, through Jesus Christ.

While still at the little church in Olney he gave the world the song that has blessed the hearts of Christians since that day.

> Amazing grace, how sweet the sound,
> That saved a wretch like me.
> I once was lost, but now am found,
> Was blind, but now I see.

17

When you sing this song, be reminded of the grace that is shown toward men whose hearts are as vile as was John Newton's. That grace is offered to you, too.

> When we've been there ten thousand years,
> Bright shining as the sun;
> We've no less days to sing God's praise
> Than when we first begun.

**REFLECTION**: Thank God for His mercy, love and grace—mercy that favors helpless ones, love that sent His Son to die for wretched ones, and grace that gives salvation to unworthy ones.

# 7

## THE DREAMER

### SCRIPTURE: Daniel 12:2-13

*And they that be wise shall shine as the brightness of the firmament; and they that turn many to righteousness as the stars for ever and ever.*

During the latter years of the nineteenth century the remains of several destroyed ships could be seen clearly at low tide a little off shore from Westwood, a small seacoast town near Boston, Massachusetts. A Baptist pastor there named Edward S. Ufford liked to stroll along the seashore and look out to sea. In his mind's eye he could see the panic-stricken victims as they desperately strove for life itself. He says, "I could see a storm, a spar, a shipwrecked sailor drifting out beyond human reach."

Later he visited several life-saving stations and watched men practice rescue techniques that all too often were needed along that rocky coast. He heard the leader bark out the order: "Throw out the lifeline!" He was shown the lifeline. Several men recounted dramatic rescues in which the lifeline was used. Those impressions, coupled with the scenes of rotting boat hulks, produced the hymn, "Throw Out the Lifeline." In a short fifteen minutes Mr. Ufford wrote these memorable words.

> Throw out the lifeline across the
>   dark wave,
> There is a brother whom someone
>   should save;
> Somebody's brother! oh, who
>   then will dare
> To throw out the lifeline, his peril to share.
>
> Chorus:
> Throw out the lifeline!
> Throw out the lifeline!
> Someone is drifting away;
> Throw out the lifeline!
> Throw out the lifeline!
> Someone is sinking today.

An interesting sequel to the story is that several years later Mr. Ufford was invited at a religious service in California to tell the story about this hymn. Now he had a real "visual aid" for the audience—a piece of the lifeline used when the *Elsie Smith* floundered and sank off Cape Cod in 1902. After the meeting, a survivor from the *Elsie Smith* came up and identified himself as being one of those who had been saved by that very lifeline.

**REFLECTION**: The greatest need in your life is to become a rescuer after you have been rescued.

# 8

## STAND!

**SCRIPTURE: Ephesians 6:10-18**

*Wherefore take unto you the whole armor of God, that ye may be able to withstand in the evil day, and having done all, to stand.*

*Stand therefore, having your loins girt about with truth, and having on the breastplate of righteousness.*

The year 1858 will long be remembered in Philadelphia as the year when great revival came and when a great gospel song was written.

Dudley A. Tyng was one of the prominent leaders in this great spiritual awakening. He was speaking, early in that year, to a crowd of five thousand men, using as his text, "Go now ye that are men, and serve the Lord" (Exod. 10:11). One report tells that conviction was so great that at the close of the service two thousand men fell to their knees. Two other writers say that at least one thousand men made confession of Christ as Savior.

A few days after that service Mr. Tyng was at work in his study. For a few moments of relaxation he decided to walk down to his barn to watch a corn-shelling machine in operation. While he patted a mule being used to operate the machine, his sleeve caught in the machine. His arm was pulled in and was so badly lacerated that it was amputated. He lived only a few days after that. Just before he died, his dad, leaning over his preacher-boy, asked him if he had any farewell words for the young men with whom he had been working. He replied, "Tell them, .... to stand up for Jesus."

George Duffield, Jr., a young pastor, was a close friend of Mr. Tyng. The Sunday following the funeral, Mr. Duffield preached a sermon exhorting his congregation to stand firm for Jesus Christ. His text was Ephesians 6:14, "Stand therefore, having your loins girt about with truth, and having on the breastplate of righteousness." At the close of the sermon he read a poem he had written.

> Stand up, stand up for Jesus,
> Ye soldiers of the cross;
> Lift high His royal banner,
> It must not suffer loss.
> From victory unto victory,
> His army shall He lead,
> Till every foe is vanquished
> And Christ is Lord indeed.

There were six stanzas in all. Benedict D. Stewart, the superintendent of the Sunday Church School, had some leaflets containing the words of that song printed for the children. A copy found its way to a Baptist paper.

Almost every hymnal today contains this great song and it has found its way into the hearts of men everywhere in many lands, causing them to have courage—courage to STAND UP FOR JESUS.

**REFLECTION:** As in 1858, our day needs men who are willing to stand up for Jesus—men who are willing to be leaders. Remember . . . when you follow the crowd you will not have a crowd following you.

# 9

## HE WOULDN'T DO IT FOR MONEY

**SCRIPTURE: Luke 18:1-14**

*And he spake a parable unto them to this end, that men ought always to pray, and not to faint.*

The town is Port Hope, Canada. A monument is being erected, not for the leading citizen who just died, but for a poor, unselfish, working man who gave most of his life and energy to help those who couldn't repay him.

Joseph Scriven was born in Dublin in 1820. In this youth Ireland had the prospect of a great citizen with high ideals and great aspirations. He was engaged to a lovely lass who had promised to share his exalted dreams. On the eve of their wedding her body was pulled from a pond into which she had accidentally fallen and drowned. Young Scriven never overcame the shock. Although a graduate of Trinity College, and ready to embark on a brilliant career, he began to wander to try to forget his sorrow. His wanderings took him to Canada where he spent the last forty-one of his sixty-six years. He became a very devout Christian.

His beliefs led him to do servile labor for poor widows and sick people. He often served for no wages.

It was not known that Mr. Scriven had any poetic gifts until a short time before his death. A friend, who was sitting with him in an illness, discovered a poem that he had written to his mother in a time of sorrow, not intending that anyone else should see it.

> What a Friend we have in Jesus,
> All our sins and griefs to bear!
> What a privilege to carry
> Everything to God in prayer!
> Oh, what peace we often forfeit,
> Oh, what needless pain we bear,
> All because we do not carry
> Everything to God in prayer.

The poem was later set to music and has become a much loved gospel song. It is said to be the first song that many missionaries teach their converts. In the polls taken to determine the popularity of hymns and gospel songs, "What a Friend We Have in Jesus" is always near the top.

Mr. Scriven will be long remembered as the man who helped others when they couldn't help themselves. If you have read other devotions in this book by now you have seen that the overriding attitude or philosophy in Christianity can be wrapped up in one word—others. We come back to it over and over again. Anything done for Christ must be done for others.

**REFLECTION**: Prayer is the most powerful force available to Christians everywhere. Any person who neglects the opportunity to commune with God and to draw on His resources will not show much growth in his faith. Reaffirm your commitment to pray more.

# 10

## LITTLE THINGS ARE IMPORTANT

**SCRIPTURE: I Peter 5:1-11**

*Casting all your care upon him; for he careth for you.*

The famous pastor and hymn writer, Robert Lowry, joined hands and hearts with one of his parishioners, Annie Sherwood Hawks, to give America and the world one of the great hymns of comfort and devotion.

One morning, in her home, Annie Hawks was happily busy about the chores at hand. She gives testimony that her home seemed to take on the light of heaven and she seemed to be in the very presence of God. The words, "I need Thee every hour," flashed into her mind. She hurriedly found pencil and paper and began to write. Phrases flowed from her pencil. In just a few moments she had completed a poem, the first stanza of which is:

> I need Thee every hour,
> Most gracious Lord.
> No tender voice like Thine
> Can peace afford.

Your life will be more dedicated to Christ when you realize that He is interested in every aspect of your being. The minutest detail of your existence is noticed by Him. Everyday tasks, like those of Mrs. Hawks, are hallowed by His concern and His presence.

Mrs. Hawks personally experienced the comforting power of her song only a few years later when her husband went to be with the Lord. She joined him in heaven in 1918.

The tune and chorus were written by Dr. Lowry. These additions have done more than a little to carry the song to a wide audience.

The song was first sung at the National Baptist Sunday School Convention in Cincinnati, Ohio, in 1872. Ira Sankey made it more popular as he used it in the Moody-Sankey meetings. It has been translated into several other languages.

Sing the second verse and chorus thoughtfully:

> I need Thee every hour,
> Stay Thou near by;
> Temptations lose their power
> When Thou art nigh.
>
> Chorus:
> I need Thee, O I need Thee;
> Every hour I need Thee!
> O bless me now, my Savior,
> I come to Thee!

**REFLECTION**: God sees you . . . NOW! He knows all about you . . . NOW! And He cares for you . . . NOW!

# 11

## BOUND WITH STRONG CORDS

**SCRIPTURE: Galatians 6:1-10**

*And let us not be weary in well doing: for in due season we shall reap, if we faint not. As we have therefore opportunity, let us do good unto all men, especially unto them who are of the household of faith.*

John Fawcett had been pastor of a small church at Wainsgate in Yorkshire, England, for seven years. His income was a small salary and his family was growing much too large to be supported by his meager wage. It seemed only practical to move to a church that paid a larger salary. A call came, and it was accepted.

Moving day soon arrived. The men were loading the preacher's furniture and books on the wagons. The last piece was loaded, and everything seemed all set for the journey. Men, women, and children stood around the wagons weeping over the loss of their beloved pastor. Seated on packed cases, the pastor and his wife could not restrain their tears. They and the church members were remembering the times when he had stood with a weeping family from whom the Lord had taken a loved one, or with a young husband anxiously awaiting the arrival of his first-born, or the times when he had taken his Bible and quietly and earnestly shown the way of salvation to a lost one, or perhaps the times when he had preached in the little church and the Holy Spirit had visited them in a special way. All of these things could not be brushed from their minds; nor did they want them to be.

Finally, Mrs. Fawcett turned to her husband and weepingly told him that she did not know how to go. He confessed that he had the same feelings. He gave the order to unload the wagons and to put everything back in its place. Out of genuine Christian love for those, his people, the preacher stayed and ministered to their needs for fifty years.

The incidents which occurred on the day he almost moved, coupled with the spirit of those kind people at Wainsgate, surely inspired him to write:

> Blest be the tie that binds
> Our hearts in Christian love;
> The fellowship of kindred minds
> Is like to that above.

**REFLECTION**: Thank God today for those pastors who labor so tirelessly among humble people, with little recompense save the knowledge that God sees them, guides them, and will supply every need.

May God give each of us the ability to stay with the task until the finish of it.

# 12

## ADORING CHRIST

**SCRIPTURE: Philippians 2:1-11**

*Wherefore God also hath highly exalted him, and given him a name which is above every name.*

I would rank this as the greatest hymn of praise in the English language:

> All hail the power of Jesus' name,
> Let angels prostrate fall;
> Bring forth the royal diadem,
> And crown Him Lord of all.

Edward Perronet, the writer of this hymn, was a close associate of John and Charles Wesley. He was born in England in 1726 and was educated for the ministry in the Church of England, following his father and grandfather in this profession. He objected to many of the practices of the church, leaning strongly to the doctrines of the Wesleys. He even advocated the starting of a new denomination, but the Wesleys would not break their ties with the Anglican Church.

Mr. Perronet was a strong, impulsive, self-willed individual; therefore, he pulled out and started an independent church in Canterbury. Shortly after Edward Perronet established his church, he wrote this famous hymn which was published in 1780 in the *Gospel Magazine* edited by Augustus Toplady. A few years later those same verses appeared in a book of poems by an anonymous author. One of the poems was written as an acrostic, the letters of which spelled Edward Perronet. Most of his work was done under an assumed name, or he used no name at all.

The tune, *Coronation,* which is just as popular as the verses, was written by one of America's most noted hymn tune writers, Oliver Holden. He composed it during a time of great rejoicing. His wife had just presented him with a fine baby girl. The four-and-a-half-octave organ on which he composed the tune is still displayed in the Old State House in Boston.

In church services today, you may hear these verses sung to three tunes: Coronation, Miles Lane or Diadem. Coronation is, by far, the most popular.

England and America came together in the persons of Edward Perronet and Oliver Holden and gave to the world the hymn, "All Hail the Power of Jesus Name."

> Let every kindred, every tribe
> On this terrestrial ball,
> To Him all majesty ascribe,
> And crown Him Lord of all.

**REFLECTION:** Christ left His majestic position and condescended to provide salvation for lowly human beings. May He enjoy an exalted position in our hearts today. He and only He is worthy to be Lord of all.

# 13

## A CONSTANT COMPANION

**SCRIPTURE: II Corinthians 13:5-11**

*Finally, brethren, farewell. Be perfect, be of good comfort, be of one mind, live in peace; and the God of love and peace shall be with you.*

If you look into the etymology of the word, *good-by,* you will find that it is a condensation of the words "God be with ye."

Dr. J. E. Rankin, former pastor of the First Congregational Church in Washington, felt the need of a song for Christians to sing as a farewell to each other. He fell to thinking of the term *good-by* and, upon learning of its origin, he began to write a poem. It began:

> God be with you till we meet again,
> By His counsels guide, uphold you,
> With His sheep securely fold you;
> God be with you till we meet again.

After he finished the first stanza, he sent it to two music composers, one a famous, well-trained musician and the other an obscure choir director. Both submitted music and the melody of the latter seemed to fit perfectly the verse.

While a student at Tennessee Temple Schools in Chattanooga, Tennessee, I had the rare privilege of helping to "send off" missionary volunteers who had graduated and were ready to do the work to which God had called them. At the depot there were always mixed emotions; some would be crying, some laughing, and some would just stand quietly. All were caught up in the solemnity of the occasion. Here was a student who had successfully completed his course of study and was now ready to go out to face the trials and hardships of the mission field. Leaving friends, family, and home seemed to fade into insignificance as the young volunteer remembered the joys that come from obeying God. As the conductor called, "B-o-o-o-a-r-d," a lump came into many throats, but the well-wishers sang as best they could. As the train slipped from sight you could hear above the click of the wheels:

> God be with you till we meet again,
> Keep love's banner flowing o'er you,
> Smite death's threatening wave before you;
> God be with you till we meet again.

**REFLECTION**: If we strengthen ourselves with the study of the Bible, we will be able to impart to others the living truth that God will be with them wherever His providence may take them. And we will impart these truths in a convincing manner.

# 14

## ALONE IN THE BIG CITY

**SCRIPTURE:** Hebrews 11:1-16

*And again, when he bringeth in the firstbegotten into the world, he saith, And let all the angels of God worship him (Heb. 1:6).*

Many of our hymns were composed as Christians wrote exactly what they felt in their hearts at the time. Such was the case in the writing of "My Faith Looks Up to Thee."

Ray Palmer, fresh out of Yale, went to New York to teach school for a while. He had a very discouraging year in which he battled illness and loneliness. One night he sat down in his room to put in verse form the feelings of his heart. He had done this sort of thing since his childhood. This night the Lord seemed particularly near and dear to him and he began to write:

> My faith looks up to Thee
> Thou Lamb of Calvary,
> Savior divine.
> Now hear me while I pray,
> Take all my guilt away,
> O let me from this day
> Be wholly Thine.

And on and on he wrote until four stanzas were completed. He copied them from the single sheet into his pocket notebook so that he could refer to them when he needed a lift. He never intended that anyone else should see them.

Several months later Ray Palmer met Dr. Lowell Mason

on a street in Boston. Dr. Mason asked him to furnish some hymns for a hymnal that he and Dr. Hastings were about to publish. For the first time Mr. Palmer displayed his poem. Dr. Mason stepped into a store and hurriedly copied the words on another sheet of paper. The words so impressed him that he wrote a tune for them, called Olivet.

A few days later the two men met again and Dr. Mason said to Mr. Palmer, "You may live many years and do many things, but I think you will be best known to posterity as the author of this song." Dr. Mason was not far wrong.

> When ends life's transient dream,
> When death's cold, sullen stream
> Would o'er me roll;
> Blest Savior, then, in love,
> Fear and distrust remove;
> O bear me safe above,
> A ransomed soul!

Your experiences with the Lord may not result in the writing of a famous hymn but they can and should be very worthwhile and very dear to you. Treasure these experiences and seek out times and places where you may be alone with the Lord.

**REFLECTION**: Ray Palmer's faith was not in himself or some "higher power." It was in Christ. Our faith also must be in Him. The Bible says that Christ was tempted in all points like as we are and yet He was without sin. In every situation that we find ourselves, Christ has been there, too.

# 15

## GOD UNDERSTANDS

**SCRIPTURE: Isaiah 35**

*And the ransomed of the Lord shall return, and come to Zion with songs and everlasting joy upon their heads: they shall obtain joy and gladness, and sorrow and sighing shall flee away.*

Tragedy struck a young missionary family when it was ready to leave Peru for a furlough in Canada. The husband and father, Clifford Bicker, was killed in an automobile accident. The tragic news traveled quickly to the bereaved wife's brother, Dr. Oswald J. Smith, who immediately sent her a poem he had written to comfort her in her hour of heartache. The name of the poem was "God Understands."

When Ruth Smith Bicker and her two fatherless children reached Canada, she told her brother of the comfort the reading of his poem had given her. He then decided to share it with others. He sent it to Mr. B. D. Ackley and asked him to write a musical setting. Mr. Ackley complied and the result was a great song of comfort, "God Understands." These are the first two stanzas:

> God understands your sorrow,
> He sees the falling tear,
> And whispers, "I am with thee,"
> Then falter not, nor fear.
>
> God understands your heartache,
> He knows the bitter pain;
> Oh, trust Him in the darkness,
> You cannot trust in vain.

Dr. Smith, the founder, and for nearly thirty years the pastor, of the Peoples Church of Toronto, Canada, traveled and preached in sixy-six foreign countries.

Yes, Dr. Smith in his lifetime did many great and wonderful things, but none were greater and more lasting than giving to the world such songs as, "Then Jesus Came," "Saved, Saved," "The Song of the Soul Set Free," and "God Understands."

**REFLECTION:** "The happiest, sweetest, tenderest homes are not those where there has been no sorrow, but those which have been overshadowed with grief, and where Christ's comfort was accepted. The very memory of the sorrow is a gentle benediction that broods ever over the household, like the silence that comes after prayer. There is a blessing sent from God in every burden of sorrow."

J. R. Miller

# 16

## SING MY SONG FOR ME

**SCRIPTURE: Psalm 23**

*The Lord is my shepherd; I shall not want. He maketh me to lie down in green pastures: he leadeth me beside the still waters.*

On the northwest corner of Broad and Arch Streets in Philadelphia stands an office building of the United Gas

Improvement Company. On the front of this building is a bronze tablet paying tribute to a great hymn and its author, Joseph Gilmore.

In 1862 Mr. Gilmore was guest speaker for a couple of Sundays and one Wednesday service at the First Baptist Church of Philadelphia. At the Wednesday evening prayer service (March 26) he used Psalm 23 as a text. He dwelt mostly on the phrase, "He leadeth me beside the still waters." The Civil War was in full swing and things looked dark. This subject was especially dear to his heart that night.

After the service Gilmore and his wife returned to the home of Deacon Wattson, next door to the church. That evening the subject of conversation was the same as that of the service—the leadership of God. As they talked, Mr. Gilmore took a pencil and paper and began to write verses. When he had finished, he handed them to his wife and thought no more of them.

Three years later he went to the Second Baptist Church of Rochester, New York, to speak as a candidate for the pastorate. Upon entering the chapel he picked up a hymnal to see what type of songs they used, and to his amazement the first song his eyes fell on was his own, written in the home of Deacon Wattson. His wife, without telling him, had sent the verses to *The Watchman and Reflector,* a paper published in Boston. William Bradbury set the verses to music. Mr. Gilmore had the people of Rochester sing the song so that he might hear how it sounded.

In 1926 the First Baptist Church of Philadelphia and Deacon Wattson's home were torn down, and an office building was constructed on that site. In memory of and appreciation for the song and its author, the gas company placed the bronze tablet on the front. The inscription begins with the first stanza of Mr. Gilmore's great song:

He leadeth me; O blessed thought!
O words with heavenly comfort fraught!
Whate'er I do, where'er I be,
Still 'tis God's hand that leadeth me.

He leadeth me, He leadeth me;
By His own hand He leadeth me.
His faithful follower I would be,
For by His hand He leadeth me.

Pause for a moment with this thought. God wants to lead you in your daily life. There are several methods He uses to give His children guidance and leadership. Among these are: the Bible, pastors, Christian counselors, circumstances and impressions from Him gained through prayer and constant openness to His will.

**REFLECTION:** Wherever He leads you, He has gone before. He, the Good Shepherd, will not lead His sheep in places too hard for them. Trust Him with every step of your life.

# 17

## CONFRONTATION

**SCRIPTURE: I John 1**

*If we confess our sins, he is faithful and just to forgive us our sins, and to cleanse us from all unrighteousness.*

How sad for a young boy to have to grow up without a dad. Robert Robinson had to because his dad passed away when Robert was only eight years of age. As soon as he was old enough, he got a job as an apprentice to a barber. Because of the hardship of having to be the breadwinner for his widowed mother and himself, his formal education was limited. However, his knowledge was varied and extensive because he spent many hours in study.

Robert Robinson was born in Norfolk, England, in September, 1735. As he grew older, he came under the influence of that great evangelist, George Whitfield. He became convicted of his terrible, sinful ways. On December 10, 1755, Robinson could not escape from a particular phrase used by Mr. Whitfield in one of his sermons: "Oh, my hearers! the wrath to come! the wrath to come!" He was wondrously converted and became a minister of the gospel; first, in a Baptist church, then in a Methodist church, and later in other denominations. Then, unfortunately, he became altogether unstable and unhappy. Some would call it "backslidden."

He found himself one day the fellow passenger of a young lady on a stagecoach. It is reported that she began to sing to break the monotony of the trip. And what did she sing?

Come, Thou fount of every blessing,
Tune my heart to sing Thy grace;
Streams of mercy, never ceasing,
Call for songs of loudest praise.
Teach me some melodious sonnet,
Sung by flaming tongues above;
Praise the mount—I'm fixed upon it—
Mount of Thy redeeming love.

She asked him what he thought about the song, and his startling reply was: "Madam, I am the unhappy man who wrote that hymn many years ago; and, I would give a thousand worlds, if I had them, if I could feel now as I felt then."

**REFLECTION**: May you never stray farther than the fingertips of the Lord; every morning and every evening come close to His heart!

# 18

## HISTORY REPEATING

**SCRIPTURE**: Luke 2:1-20

*Glory to God in the highest, and on earth peace, good will toward men.*

Never a poet put pen to paper with more skill in verse than Henry Wadsworth Longfellow. His ability to portray life in one of the most beautiful fashions ever devised—poetry—is illustrated in his masterful, "The Song of Hiawatha."

Longfellow was a legend in his own lifetime. He is known in many circles as "The Children's Poet." In his last years, in many schools, his birthday was a holiday and school children were excused from classes.

Longfellow is not usually thought of as a hymn writer, but one of his poems has been set to music by an Englishman, John Calkin, and the result is one of our most popular Christmas carols.

On Christmas Day, 1863, Longfellow wrote of the joys of the season: (sing each stanza as you come to it.)

> I heard the bells on Christmas day
> Their old familiar carols play,
> And wild and sweet the words repeat
> Of peace on earth, good will to men.

As he came to the third stanza he was stopped by the thought of the condition of his beloved country. The Civil War was in full swing. The battle of Gettysburg was not more than six months past. Days looked dark, and he probably asked himself the question, "How can the last phrase of those stanzas to be true in this war-torn country, where brother fights against brother and father against son?" But he kept writing:

> And in despair I bowed my head:
> "There is no peace on earth," I said,
> "For hate is strong, and mocks the song
> Of peace on earth, good will to man!"

It seems as if he could have been writing for the present day, too.

Then, as every Christian should do, he turned his thoughts to the one who solves all problems:

> Then pealed the bells more loud and deep:
> "God is not dead, nor doth He sleep;
> The wrong shall fail, the right prevail,
> With peace on earth, good will to men."

Millions of children and adults alike the world over love this carol.

**REFLECTION**: Peace and good will, will one day come when the Prince of Peace shall reign. Peace in this life, for a Christian, is from within, not in an exemption from suffering.

# 19

## A TRULY GREAT MAN

### SCRIPTURE: I Timothy 6:7-16

*Fight the good fight of faith, lay hold on eternal life, whereunto thou art also called, and hast professed a good profession before many witnesses.*

On a holiday known as Whitmonday (seven weeks after Easter) the children of Sabine Baring-Gould's Sunday school were invited to join celebrations in the neighboring town of Yorkshire. Baring-Gould thought that the children should have a song to sing as they marched along carrying their crosses and banners on the way to Yorkshire but he could not find an appropriate song. He sat up most of the night before the holiday, writing verses. By morning he had completed a song. He taught it to the children the next day, using as a melody the theme from Haydn's Symphony in D. As they marched along the children sang:

> Onward, Christian soldiers,
> Marching as to war,
> With the cross of Jesus
> Going on before:
> Christ, the royal Master,
> Leads against the foe;
> Forward into battle,
> See His banners go.

This song, like many others, has gone farther than the writer ever hoped or dreamed. Everywhere, in every country of the world, one may hear the strains of this great Christian march.

No longer is Haydn's theme used, but a wonderful composition by Sir Arthur Sullivan, of Gilbert and Sullivan fame.

The song as it is now, with Sullivan's music and Baring-Gould's verses, is a soul-stirring, fighting song, for real "soldiers of the cross."

> Onward, then, ye people!
> Join our happy throng!
> Blend with ours your voices
> In the triumph song!
> Glory, laud and honor,
> Unto Christ the King;
> This through countless ages
> Men and angels sing.

Many of the great song writers of the past have been men of renowned literary ability. So was Sabine Baring-Gould. He wrote and published eighty-five books on many different subjects in his lifetime. Included in these are books on theology, travel, history, myths, and the origin of folk tunes.

He fell in love with a young lady of his congregation named Grace Taylor. She was the daughter of a poor mill hand. With the consent of her parents he sent her away to school to be educated. Upon her return they were united in marriage in a most impressive ceremony with Baring-Gould himself pronouncing the vows. They became the parents of fifteen children. When she died, eight years before his death, he had engraved on her tombstone, "Half of my soul."

**REFLECTION**: Sabine Baring-Gould was a man of marvelous Christian character. He saw what needed to be done, set out to do it, and was unusually successful. He just kept pushing on for God and the result was a life of tremendous usefulness.

# 20

## DO IT AGAIN, LORD!

**SCRIPTURE: John 6:29-40**

*For the bread of God is he which cometh down from heaven, and giveth life unto the world.*

One morning a small lad left home with five barley loaves and two small fishes. During the course of the day he and his food became a significant part of one of the best known miracles that Jesus performed: The feeding of the five thousand.

Later, the Scriptural account of this glorious miracle of our Lord gave rise to a much-loved gospel song, a song written by Mary Artemisia Lathbury.

Dr. John Vincent (later Bishop Vincent of the Methodist Church) instituted the Chautauqua Assembly, a Methodist camp meeting grounds on Lake Chautauqua in New York. One facet of the Chautauqua Assembly was the Chautauqua Literary and Scientific Circle. During the encampment of 1877, Dr. Vincent asked Miss Lathbury to write a song that could be used as a study song during the sessions. The result was the beautiful and ever popular, "Break Thou the Bread of Life." Almost every hymnal today contains this hymn:

> Break Thou the bread of life,
> Dear Lord, to me,
> As Thou did'st break the loaves
> Beside the sea;
> Beyond the sacred page
> I seek Thee, Lord;
> My spirit pants for Thee,

**REFLECTION:** We are blest indeed when we stop to feed our souls with the "bread of God." As Jesus, through a lad, shared with thousands He was giving us a valuable lesson—sharing Christ with others. Many are famishing in a world of spiritual hunger. We must do what we can to help.

# 21

## A PRAYER THAT BECAME A SONG

**SCRIPTURE: I Corinthians 10:1-13**

*And did all drink the same spiritual drink: for they drank of that spiritual Rock that followed them: and that Rock was Christ.*

*"A Living and Dying Prayer for the Holiest Believer in the World."* This was the first title for one of the most loved of all hymns, "Rock of Ages." Few hymns, if any, have a similar background. It was born out of argumentation, debate, and criticism.

The author, Augustus Montague Toplady, was very frail. His body held up for only thirty-eight years under the strain of his fiery zeal. He tells that he was converted at the age of sixteen under the ministry of a poor preacher who could scarcely write his name. His conversion took place in Ireland in a service held in a barn with only a few people present.

He, an avowed Calvinist, fell into controversy with John Wesley, the then champion of the Arminians. The battle waged long and hot between these two theologians, even though Wesley had obtained prominence in England and was fifty years Toplady's senior.

The poem that we now know as "Rock of Ages" was a part of this debate. It is interesting to know that Toplady published a book of songs and included in it "Jesus, Lover of My Soul," by—you guessed it—John Wesley.

> Rock of Ages, cleft for me,
> Let me hide myself in Thee;
> Let the water and the blood,
> From Thy wounded side which flowed,
> Be of sin the double cure,
> Save from its guilt and power.

You see, Augustus Toplady and John Wesley were very strongly opposed to the other's theology but each maintained his Christian character and his love for the other. It is one thing to disagree and quite another to be disagreeable. You and I could disagree "agreeably" with our Christian brothers and remain friends.

**REFLECTION:** Some of your friends may be people who disagree with many of your actions, philosophy, and standards. Listen to them, take their advice, and then through the Holy Scripture be led of God.

# 22

## BLIND FANNY THINKS OF OTHERS

**SCRIPTURE: Psalm 126**

*He that goeth forth and weepeth, bearing precious seed, shall doubtless come again with rejoicing, bringing his sheaves with him.*

Fanny Crosby was deeply interested in gospel work among poor men who were down and out. One evening in New York she addressed a large company of men in the slum area. Her heart was moved at the close of her address as she heard a young boy, eighteen years of age come forward and say, "I promised my mother to meet her in heaven, but the way I am now living, that will be impossible." After prayer was offered for him, he arose with a new light in his eyes. He exclaimed that since he had now found God, he would be meeting his mother in heaven. As the service continued, her poetic mind began to work, and before she retired at home that evening she had completed the verses to a "battle cry" for the great army of Christian soldiers. Think of the lost as you sing:

> Rescue the perishing,
> Care for the dying,
> Snatch them in pity from sin and the grave;
> Weep o'er the erring one,
> Lift up the fallen,
> Tell them of Jesus the mighty to save.

The Moody and Sankey meetings helped to popularize many of Fanny Crosby's eight thousand hymns and gospel songs in this country and in England. Her motto was, "I think that life is not too long, and therefore I determine that many people read a song who would not read a sermon."

Frances Jane Crosby was born in Putnam County, New York, on March 24, 1820. Her sight was destroyed at the age of six weeks because of the misapplication of a poultice on her eyes. She was blessed with a wonderful disposition and accepted her handicap with an unusual display of courage.

Fanny Crosby was born the second time in 1851. Seven years later she married a blind musician, Mr. Alexander Van Alstyne.

Her cheerfulness and courage coupled with simple, childlike trust in divine watch-care enabled her to write such heartwarming hymns as "Blessed Assurance," "Jesus, Keep Me Near the Cross" and "Safe in the Arms of Jesus."

Friday morning, February 12, 1915, just prior to her ninety-fifth birthday, Fanny Crosby realized to the fullest the words she had written and recited many times—"and I shall see HIM face to face."

**REFLECTION**: Here is another example of a person who would not sit down and feel sorry for herself. In her blindness she thought constantly of others. We, like she, can find peace only as we turn aside to help someone else and then happiness seems to overtake us.

# 23

## THE NIGHT THE LIGHTS WENT OUT

**SCRIPTURE**: Matthew 5:1-17

*Let your light so shine before men, that they may see your good works and glorify your Father which is in heaven.*

This story is probably a familiar one, but it will bear repeating because it, like the hymn, wears like steel.

Philip Bliss was in the congregation of Dwight L. Moody when he heard him tell this story: "On a dark stormy night, when the waves rolled like mountains and not a star was to be seen, a boat, rocking and plunging, neared the Cleveland harbor. 'Are you sure this is Cleveland?' asked the captain, seeing only one light from the lighthouse.

'Quite sure, sir,' replied the pilot.

'Where are the lower lights?'

'Gone out, sir.'

'Can you make the harbor?'

'We must, or perish, sir!'

"With a strong hand and a brave heart the old pilot turned the wheel. But, alas, in the darkness he missed the channel, and with a crash upon the rocks the boat was shivered, and many a life was lost in a watery grave. Brethren, the Master will take care of the great lighthouse; let us keep the lower lights burning!"

As he sat there, the heart of P. P. Bliss was touched deeply. His alert mind began to work rapidly, and at the very next service he sang a new song. The first stanza and chorus went like this:

> Brightly beams our Father's mercy
> From His lighthouse evermore,

But to us He gives the keeping
Of the lights along the shore,

Chorus:
Let the lower lights be burning!
Send a gleam across the wave!
Some poor fainting, struggling seaman
You may rescue, you may save.

God has allowed only a few to write these wonderful gospel songs, but He has allowed millions in many lands to sing songs like, "Let the Lower Lights Be Burning."

**REFLECTION**: Often our lights flicker, grow dim, and go out without our being aware of it. Others read our lives. We didn't choose that situation but it is, nevertheless, a reality. We will give account as to how we lead people in this world.

# 24

## TALKING WITH THE LORD

**SCRIPTURE: Ephesians 6:10-24**

*Praying always with all prayer and supplication in the Spirit, and watching thereunto with all perseverance and supplication for all saints.*

"Now I lay me down to sleep, I pray the Lord my soul to keep. If I should die before I wake, I pray the Lord my soul to take." This and other childhood prayers began to pass through the mind of Mosie Lister one wintery day in 1956. "How long has it been since some people have talked with the Lord?" he asked himself. "Some of us prayed in younger years, but have gotten away from that childhood faith." He picked up a pencil and paper and phrases began to flow as fast as he could write them down. A tune came with them. In about fifteen minutes a song was written.

As you may have already guessed, the title of the song is "How Long Has It Been?" With Mr. Lister's permission, the first stanza is quoted here:

How long has it been since you talked with the Lord,
And told Him your heart's hidden secrets?
How long since you prayed? How long since you stayed
On your knees till the light shone through?
How long has it been since your mind felt at ease?
How long since your heart knew no burden?
Can you call Him your friend? How long has it been,
Since you knew that He cared for you?

Since 1955, after several different jobs in the music field and a hitch in the Navy, Mosie Lister has devoted his life to the writing of gospel songs and hymns. Mr. Lister told me about his hymn writing one day in Tampa, Florida, several years ago. Then he added: "I think that God has directed my thoughts on certain occasions toward writing songs. I don't think my songs would have gone as well as they have if God hadn't directed. I prayed that God would use what talent I have to bring some blessing to other people."

**REFLECTION:** What was your answer to the question in this song? How long . . . how long since you really were burdened about a friend or loved one and prayed until God heard and answered? How long . . . how long since you rose from your knees a victorious Christian? Make today your day to renew your vow to pray as you ought. Take advantage of this wonderful power in your life!

# 25

## WHAT THE TUNE SAID

**SCRIPTURE: Psalm 16**

*Thou wilt shew me the path of life: in thy presence is fulness of joy; at thy right hand there are pleasures for evermore.*

In 1868 William Howard Doane made a quick business trip to New York. He hurriedly took care of the business matter and rushed on to Brooklyn to the home of Fanny Crosby. He found her talking to Mr. William Bradbury, one of the great sacred song writers of the past. Doane told her that he had written a tune and that he wanted her to hear it. He played it for her on a small organ. When he had finished she excitedly exclaimed that the tune said, "safe in the arms of Jesus."

She quickly went to another room and in a matter of minutes had composed the words to what became her favorite hymn. Little did she realize the peace and joy that would be brought to many hearts by this great song.

For many years this song has been used at funerals, but Fanny Crosby did not mean for it to be used primarily in that way. You can be sure that it was her prayer that everyone who heard her song would soon be able to sing with her:

Safe in the arms of Jesus,
Safe on His gentle breast,
There by His love o'ershaded,
Sweetly my soul shall rest.
Hark! 'tis the voice of angels,
Borne in a song to me,
Over the fields of glory,
Over the jasper sea.

Jesus, my heart's dear refuge,
Jesus has died for me;
Firm on the Rock of Ages,
Ever my trust shall be.
Here let me wait with patience,
Wait till the night is o'er;
Wait till I see the morning,
Break on the golden shore.

Chorus:
Safe in the arms of Jesus,
Safe on His gentle breast,
There by His love o'ershaded,
Sweetly my soul shall rest.

**REFLECTION**: Because Fanny Crosby lived close to God, God allowed her on a moment's notice to be a blessing to multiplied thousands who would live even after her death. Oh, that we would so live that when we come to the end of our lives we can look back and see that on numerous occasions we were able to be a blessing to others because we kept our hearts in tune with God.

# 26

## A HIT FROM THE START

**SCRIPTURE: Luke 21:20-33**

*And then shall they see the Son of man coming in a cloud with power and great glory.*

Very seldom do the people of the world pick a sacred song, done in a simple yet beautiful way, and make a "hit" of it. But such has been the case with Julia Ward Howe's, "The Battle Hymn of the Republic."

This song, born out of the Civil War and set to the tune of "John Brown's Body," is a great contribution by a very talented woman.

During the Civil War the soldiers used the song, "John Brown's Body," as a marching tune. It has a snappy rhythm. Mrs. Howe heard this tune many times and often prayed that she might write more suitable words for such a melody.

With her husband and some friends, she rode just outside Washington one day to watch the reviewing of some army troops. During the course of the day she heard the soldiers singing the song mentioned above. One of her companions turned and asked her why she didn't write some good words to that tune.

In recounting the story of her song, she said that she awakened the next morning before dawn thinking of the tune and framing verses in her mind. She sprang out of bed and quickly wrote the verses on a piece of paper.

She lived nearly a century and did some wonderful things for which she is still remembered—but she is most famous for writing "The Battle Hymn of the Republic." surely you can sing this!

Mine eyes have seen the glory
    of the coming of the Lord:
He is trampling out the vintage
    where the grapes of wrath are stored;
He hath loosed the fateful lightning
    of His terrible swift sword;
His truth is marching on.

Chorus:
Glory! glory, hallelujah!
Glory! glory, hallelujah!
Glory! glory, hallelujah!
His truth is marching on.

**REFLECTION**: The great God that we serve, magnified in this song, is not only a God of terrible wrath against those who disobey Him, but also a God of divine justice and unending truth. Great men, as the world counts greatness, live and die and are acclaimed for a while. But God continues to march on. Isn't it wonderful to know that He sees us, He knows all about us, and He cares for us?

# 27

## FROM RAGS TO RICHES

**Mark 10:43-52**

*And Jesus said unto him, Go thy way; thy faith hath made thee whole. And immediately he received his sight, and followed Jesus in the way.*

One day Dr. Oswald J. Smith, former pastor of the People's Church of Toronto, Canada, was at the Rodeheaver Music Company listening to Mr. B. D. Ackley play the piano when in walked Homer Rodeheaver, the dean of song leaders. Mr. Rodeheaver has recently heard a sermon by Harry Rimmer, in which he vividly described the beggar beside the roadway, shrinking in the shadows of poverty with his clothes clutched about him. When Christ came the beggar was able to unfurl his arms, signifying the liberating power of Jesus Christ. Mr. Rodeheaver was so impressed that he said to Dr. Smith, "Oswald, I want you to write me a poem telling of the change that takes place in a life after Jesus comes in." Dr. Smith consented to do so, returned to his office at the China Inland Mission headquarters, and finished the poem.

The next day he gave the verses to Mr. Rodeheaver who wrote a wonderful musical setting that is said to be his best musical composition.

You have probably already guessed that the song was "Then Jesus Came."

> One sat alone, beside the highway begging,
> His eyes were blind, the light he could not see;
> He clutched his rags and shivered in the shadows,
> Then Jesus came and bade his darkness flee.

Chorus:
When Jesus comes, the tempter's power is broken;
When Jesus comes, the tears are wiped away.
He takes the gloom and fills the life with glory,
For all is changed when Jesus comes to stay.

**REFLECTION**: When Christ comes into a life, He sets the captive free. "Old things are passed away, behold all things are become new." The gambler is freed from his compulsion to wager, the thief no longer steals, the liar becomes fanatically truthful, and the harlot is made as white as snow. Who rules your life?

# 28

## SEEING THROUGH OTHERS' EYES

### SCRIPTURE: Revelation 22:1-9

*And there shall be no night there; and they need no candle, neither light of the sun; for the Lord God giveth them light: and they shall reign for ever and ever.*

On April 16, 1961, I had the privilege of visiting with Mr. and Mrs. Virgil P. Brock of Winona Lake, Indiana. Mr. Brock told the story behind his renowned gospel song, "Beyond The Sunset."

"We were watching a sunset over Winona Lake one evening. With us was a couple, Horace and Grace Pierce

Burr. Horace had been blind for many years, but he talked about that sunset with us, and we went to the dinner table still talking about that impressive sunset. The lake just seemed to blaze with the glory of God. But above that unusual sunset were threatening storm clouds. As we talked about that sunset, Horace remarked, even though he was blind, 'I never saw a more beautiful sunset, and I've seen them around the world.'

"I said, 'Horace, you always talk about seeing.'

"He said, 'I do. I see through others' eyes, and I think I see more than many others see. I can see beyond the sunset.'

"I said, 'Horace, that's a great idea for a gospel song and I began singing:

> Beyond the sunset, O blissful morning,
> When with our Savior heaven is begun.'

"Cousin Grace spoke up excitedly and said, 'Oh, Blanche, that's a beautiful thought. Go and play it.'

"Mrs. Brock laid down her fork and went around to the piano close by and began to play. We stopped eating and listened as she finished the entire musical theme. She came back to the table and began eating again. I was too excited to eat. I found an old envelope in my pocket and laid it by my plate. We soon had the first verse. (He began singing.)

> Beyond the sunset, O blissful morning,
> When with our Savior heaven is begun.
> Earth's toiling ended, O glorious dawning,
> Beyond the sunset, when day is done.

"Then, remembering those threatening storm clouds gave rise to the second verse:

Beyond the sunset no clouds will gather,
No storms will threaten, no fears annoy;
O day of gladness, O day unending,
Beyond the sunset, eternal joy!

"Then I said, 'Horace, we ought to have a verse of this song for you and Grace. She has guided you about for so many years in your blindness, with her hand on yours. How would this do?

Beyond the sunset a hand will guide me
To God, the Father, whom I adore;
His glorious presence, His words of welcome,
Will be my portion on that fair shore.' "

"Beyond The Sunset" has become one of the most widely used gospel songs in print today.

**REFLECTION**: This life with Christ is wonderful . . . and heaven awaits us! As blind Horace Burr needed a hand to guide him, so we too, who were blinded by sin, have been guided by the hand of God, to life through His Son. Because of this miracle of the new birth, with Horace we can see beyond the sunset.

# 29

## MY SUNBEAM

**SCRIPTURE: Matthew 18:1-14**

*Even so it is not the will of your Father which is in heaven, that one of these little ones should perish.*

Among the poor and suffering, Elizabeth Clephane was known as "My Sunbeam." She was born in Edinburgh in 1830. At an early age she learned the meaning of sorrow, through the loss of her parents. She was a very bright child with a vivid imagination and a passionate love for poetry. She was first in her class and was, as it is reported, a favorite pupil of her teacher.

As she grew older she gave all of her money beyond the bare necessities to charities.

For a friend, she wrote a poem which found its way to a newspaper. Ira Sankey purchased a copy of the paper as he was traveling with D. L. Moody through Scotland. They were on their way to Edinburgh for three days of meetings.

As Mr. Sankey rode along he read the newspaper and cast it aside to pick it up again just as the journey was ending. He saw a poem in one corner of the paper, which he read with great interest and admiration. He clipped it and slipped it into his vest pocket, the seed-plot from which sprang many gospel songs that are now known throughout the world.

At the noon meeting on the second day, Mr. Moody presented a message titled, "The Good Shepherd." At the end of his message he called on Dr. Bonar to say a few words. When Dr. Bonar was finished, Mr. Moody turned to Mr. Sankey and asked if he had an appropriate song for the close of the service. Frantically, Mr. Sankey began to search for a song. He suddenly thought of the poem that he had stuffed in his vest pocket. He stepped to the small organ, his hands fell on the keys, he struck an A flat chord, and composing as he went, he began to sing for the first time, "The Ninety and Nine." The words and music remain unchanged.

A short time later, Mr. Sankey received a letter from Elizabeth Clephane's sister thanking him for singing the words written by Elizabeth who had already gone to be with her Shepherd.

> There were ninety and nine
>     that safely lay
> In the shelter of the fold,
> But one was out on the hills away,
> Far off from the gates of gold—
> Away on the mountains wild and bare,
> Away from the tender Shepherd's care.
>
> But all through the mountains,
>     thunder riven,
> And up from the rocky steep,
> There arose a glad cry to the gates of heaven,
> "Rejoice! I have found my sheep!"
> And the angels echoed around the throne,
> "Rejoice, for the Lord brings back His own."

**REFLECTION**: Perhaps the most wonderful thing about the Christian religion is that you as an individual are important in the eyes of God.

# 30

## THE STORY WANTED . . . THE STORY TOLD

**SCRIPTURE: Matthew 28:1-20**

*Go ye therefore, and teach all nations, baptizing them
in the name of the Father, and of the Son, and of the
Holy Ghost.*

When Katherine (Kate) Hankey passed away in 1911,
many of her former Sunday school pupils—pupils she had
taught fifty years earlier—traveled long distances to attend
her funeral. This gives some indication of the tremendous
influence that this lady carried.

At the age of eighteen she began her work for Christ by
starting a Sunday school class for shopgirls and later she
also started one for those of her own social standing. She
was a banker's daughter. From both classes came many
people who yielded themselves to God and His service.

In January of 1866 she became quite ill and spent many
months convalescing. During this recovery period she wrote
a poem that she later called "The Old, Old Story." At first
she wrote only eight stanzas of four lines each and called
them, "The Story Wanted." Later that year, in November,
she finished the poem, bringing the number of stanzas to
fifty and called the second part, "The Story Told." It is
said that any number of hymns could be chosen from the
many verses.

In 1867, in Montreal, at a convention of the Young
Men's Christian Association, William H. Doane saw Major
General Russell of the English forces stand and read the
poem with tears streaming down his bronzed cheeks. Doane
was so moved that he wrote a musical setting for the poem.
He called the song, "Tell Me The Old, Old Story."

Tell me the old, old story,
Of unseen things above,
Of Jesus and His glory,
Of Jesus and His love;

Tell me the story simply,
As to a little child,
For I am weak and weary,
And helpless and defiled.

Chorus:
Tell me the old, old, story,
Tell me the old, old, story,
Tell me the old, old, story,
Of Jesus and His love.

Little did he realize at the time that it would be sung by millions in many lands and be translated into many languages.

Miss Hankey once made a trip to Africa to take care of her invalid brother who had gone there as a missionary. During her stay in this darkened continent she became so burdened for foreign missions that she gave all of the royalties from her publications to mission work.

**REFLECTION**: It is not surprising that one whose life was marked by unselfishness and yielding to others would leave to the world a song like the one we have just sung. It is an "old, old story," but one that is so magnificent and life-giving that each time it is repeated, it seems to be new.

# 31

## A SIMPLE, WONDERFUL THING

### SCRIPTURE: I Corinthians 6:12-20

*For ye are bought with a price: therefore glorify God in your body, and in your spirit, which are God's.*

"If God has no more service for me to do through grace, I am ready; it is a great mercy to me that I have no manner of fear or dread of death. I could, if God pleases, lay my head back and die without alarm this afternoon or night. My chief supports are from my view of eternal things, and my sins are pardoned through the blood of Jesus Christ." Those are the words of a man who holds one of the highest positions among hymn writers. His name is Isaac Watts.

Isaac Watts was born July 17, 1674, at Southampton, England. He was born into the home of "non-Conformists" in the days when Dissenters and Independents were persecuted by the Church of England. Fortunately this intolerance lasted only a short while after his birth. His father, twice jailed during the persecution, afterward prospered in his business and was able to give his son the best kind of education. Isaac entered the ministry and preached his first sermon at the age of twenty-four.

His utter lack of what is commonly known as handsomeness was probably responsible for the fact that he remained unmarried throughout his life. Yet I'm sure this frail soul had learned the truth of the verse which begins this meditation.

He wrote many scholarly papers that were used in several institutions of higher learning. Yet one of the most memorable pieces that came from his pen was a simple hymn, "Alas! and Did My Savior Bleed."

Fanny Crosby testified that this song helped her to find the Savior when "believing" came most difficult. Countless other individuals have been blessed and helped by this masterful composition.

> Alas! and did my Savior bleed,
> And did my Sovereign die?
> Would He devote that sacred head
> For such a worm as I?

**REFLECTION**: May every step of our existence be guided by the stark realization that we can be in God's will only as we yield to Him that which He rightfully owns . . . our lives.

# 32

## GIVE ME ALL IN THIS HOUSE

### SCRIPTURE: Romans 12:1-16

*I beseech you therefore, brethren, by the mercies of God, that ye present your bodies a living sacrifice, holy, acceptable unto God, which is your reasonable service.*

"Splendid! To be so near the gates of heaven." Those were farewell words of a short but useful life, that of Frances Ridley Havergal.

Miss Havergal was born in Ashley, Worcestershire, in

1836. She showed an aptitude for poetry when she was only seven. She later trained in music, becoming proficient in playing the piano. She was very healthy and strong in her younger years but in her early twenties became ill and was confined to a wheelchair most of the rest of her life. Even in those trying years she kept a cheerful attitude and was able to be a blessing to those with whom she came in contact. It is reported that she never once complained of her infirmities.

One of her most popular songs came as a result of a visit to London for five days. She visited a home in which was a family of ten persons. Shortly after arriving she found that several members of the household were unconverted, while others were not rejoicing Christians. She asked God to give her all in the house before she left.

On the last night of her stay, the governess brought the two daughters to her, weeping. They were both deeply concerned about their spiritual welfare and were asking to see Miss Havergal. She was able to lead them to Christ. These two made the family circle complete. Miss Havergal later confessed that she stayed up most of the night rejoicing and reconsecrating her life to God. As the hours with God wore on, the lines of a poem began to form in her mind. They came in couplets, something like this:

> Take my life and let it be
> Consecrated, Lord, to Thee.
> Take my moments and my days,
> Let them flow in endless praise.

This hymn, coming out of a great period of devotion in her life, is probably our greatest song of consecration.

> Take my will and make it Thine;
> It shall be no longer mine.

Take my heart, it is Thine own;
It shall be Thy royal throne.

Take my love; my Lord, I pour
At Thy feet its treasure store;
Take myself, and I will be,
Ever, only, all for Thee.

**REFLECTION**: How refreshing it is to read of one like Miss Havergal, who was so infirm that she was confined to a wheelchair. Yet her thoughts were continually of others. Whatever your condition, it can be brighter and more cheerful if your thoughts will turn to others. Live in such a way that in your sunset years you can look back and see that someone was helped, some life was made better, because you cared and helped.

# 33

## THE POWER OF SONG

### SCRIPTURE: Hebrews 11:1-16

*But without faith it is impossible to please him: for he that cometh to God must believe that he is, and that he is a rewarder of them that diligently seek him.*

It was on a cold, windy night that a man named Conrad heard a lad singing as he walked by his house. Conrad invited him in, gave him something to eat, and let him warm himself. Arrangements were made for the boy to live with them. They loved him, cared for him, and sent him to school. He graduated with a Doctor of Philosophy degree.

He entered the Catholic priesthood and tried to serve well, but he could never find peace of heart and soul. He thought, "If only I could make the pilgrimage to Rome, these fears would vanish." He did make that pilgrimage. While crawling up Pilate's Staircase on his knees, he remembered the verse of Scripture, "The just shall live by Faith." He sprang to his feet and the "REFORMATION" began.

Later, to the amazement of everyone, Martin Luther started writing hymns and gospel songs. The people loved them so dearly that the Catholic ecclesiastics said that the songs of Martin Luther were destroying more souls than all his writing and sermons. He preached long and hard and became a forceful leader of one of the world's greatest revivals.

On his tomb is inscribed, "A Mighty Fortress Is Our God." That is the name of his famous hymn. It is said to be "the greatest hymn of the greatest man in the greatest period in German history."

It is a paraphrase of the Forty-sixth Psalm. The first stanza is:

> A mighty fortress is our God,
> A bulwark never failing;
> Our Helper He, amid the flood
> Of mortal ills prevailing.
> For still our ancient foe
> Doth seek to work us woe;
> His craft and power are great,
> And armed with cruel hate,
> On earth is not his equal.

Frederick H. Hedge translated it from the German in

1853. Christians have been singing it for over four hundred years and it is still a soul-stirring hymn.

**REFLECTION**: To have faith in God is a Christian's greatest asset. Faith enables one to do his best for God at all times. It is really an evidence of true love for Him.

# 34

## TO THE DOWN-AND-OUTER

**SCRIPTURE: Matthew 16:6-20**

*And I say also unto thee, That thou art Peter, and upon this rock I will build my church; and the gates of hell shall not prevail against it.*

Stainless in character, strong in body, steady in nerve, studious in learning, and swift to the defense of the gospel are said to be characteristics of one Samuel John Stone, born in England in 1839.

His tender heart led him to the down-and-outer, the man on the other side of the tracks. He was a great leader of his people and was loved by them all.

Even in his later years he enjoyed a remarkable ministry among the shop hands and office workers of London. As the early, cheaper trains began to stream into the city bringing the workers, Samuel Stone would open his church and have periods of singing and short messages for the people. He then would allow them to sit quietly and visit, sew, or read until it was time for them to begin their day's work.

He noted that many used the "Apostle's Creed" in their praying, but that few of them had any comprehension of its meaning. This ignorance, coupled with the blasphemy of the evolutionist and materialist of his day, prompted Stone to write one of the truly great hymns used in our churches today, "The Church's One Foundation."

> The Church's one foundation
> Is Jesus Christ her Lord;
> She is His new creation
> By water and the Word:
> From Heaven He came and sought her
> To be His holy bride;
> With His own blood He bought her,
> And for her life He died.

No hymn could be more Scriptural. In the first stanza the writer tells that the foundation of Christ's Church is Himself, that a man must be born of water and the Word, and that Christ gave Himself for His Church and purchased her with His own blood.

**REFLECTION**: It is not enough to know about Christ. In order to go to heaven we must know Him and we must become His. When we give Christ His rightful place, the rest of our theology seems to fall in place.

# 35

## GRATITUDE

**SCRIPTURE**: Ephesians 5:1-21

*Giving thanks always for all things unto God and the Father in the name of our Lord Jesus Christ.*

"I do this day in the presence of God and my own soul renew my covenant with God and solemnly determine henceforth to become His and to do His work as far as in me lies." These astounding words of determination came from a lad, sixteen years of age, in England, in 1826. His name was Henry Alford. He came from a long line of clergymen. His father, his grandfather and his great-grandfather were all ministers of the Church of England before him. He, too, became an Anglican vicar.

Henry Alford was born in London in 1810 and was reared in that great city. His first charge, after graduation from Trinity College, Cambridge, was in Wymeswold, Leicestershire. His gentle disposition, cheerful attitude, and sheer genius catapulted him to fame and high honor. He reached the "top" in 1857 when he became the Dean of Canterbury Cathedral.

He was a versatile man: an artist, an organist and singer, composer of verse, and superb preacher. His literary ability was climaxed with the completion of his *The Greek Testament,* a commentary of four volumes, which required twenty years of hard labor.

It is reported that he loved to mingle with the common man. He never seemed to lose his vision of the pit from which he, too, had been lifted. He was thankful. While he was at Wymeswold, his first charge, and in the fall of 1844, the people of this hamlet decided to have a harvest festival, rejoicing in the abundant harvest already gathered into their barns. For this particular occasion Mr. Alford wrote a song which has been used since at Thanksgiving time.

Come, ye thankful people, come,
Raise the song of harvest-home:
All is safely gathered in,
Ere the winter storms begin;
God, our Maker, doth provide
For our wants to be supplied:
Come to God's own temple, come,
Raise the song of harvest-home.

**REFLECTION**: After you sing this inspiring song, rededicate yourself to a life of thankfulness. Learn to see and appreciate the little things that you so often overlook. Try to talk to God for fifteen minutes, thanking Him, and refraining from asking anything for yourself.

# 36

## BLIND FAITH?

**SCRIPTURE: Philippians 4:6-23**

*But my God shall supply all your need according to his riches in glory by Christ Jesus.*

Those who knew Fanny Crosby, heard her many times over greet her friends with, "God bless your dear soul."

Even though she was blind from six weeks old, she lived a life of cheerfulness. She once declared she thought that on the whole it had been a good thing that she had been blind. She said that in the case of the loss of her sight, she could see how the Lord permitted it. She felt that the Lord didn't order it, but did permit it to happen. A favorite text was "What I do thou knowest not now, but thou shalt know hereafter." She often quoted:

> His purposes will ripen fast,
> Unfolding every hour;
> The bud may have a bitter taste,
> But sweet will be the flower.

She lived almost a century. In her ninety-four years she wrote eight thousand Christian songs and hymns, and scattered sunshine and happiness wherever she went.

On one occasion she needed a small amount of cash. She did not have time to contact her publishers to ask for an advance, so she knelt in prayer, asking God to supply her need. When she had finished praying, she arose and began to walk back and forth in her room, trying to get into a mood to write another hymn. She was under contract with her publishers to write three hymns each week.

Suddenly—a knock at the door! She greeted her visitor with her usual, "God bless your dear soul." After a few minutes of visiting with her, the guest arose and started to leave. In bidding her good-by, he shook hands with her and left in her hand the exact amount she needed. Immediately she knelt again, this time thanking God for answering her prayer. She arose from her prayer, her heart bubbling with joy and inspired to write:

> All the way my Savior leads me;
> What have I to ask beside?

Can I doubt His tender mercy,
Who through life has been my Guide?

Heavenly peace, divinest comfort,
Here by faith in Him to dwell!
For I know, what'er befall me,
Jesus doeth all things well.

**REFLECTION**: God knows our needs and He will supply if
we trust Him. He sends the times of wanting so that we
may enjoy the times of plenty. He sends the clouds so that
we can better appreciate the sunshine. He sends us into the
valley so that we may recognize His mountain peaks of rich
blessings.

# 37

## TRUE GREATNESS

**SCRIPTURE: Philippians 4:1-9**

*Those things, which ye have both learned, and re-
ceived, and heard, and seen in me, do: and the God of
peace shall be with you.*

When the roll of great preachers is sometimes called, the
name of Elisha A. Hoffman is usually omitted. As men
count greatness, this omission is justified, but E.A. Hoffman was nonetheless a mighty servant of God. Almost two
thousand gospel songs and hymns came from his pen. When

not working in his study, he could often be found working with the poor in the homes across the tracks.

One day he visited a home of one of his parishioners in the hills of Lebanon, Pennsylvania. Sorrow and affliction were frequent visitors at this home, too. He found the mother in the depths of sorrow and despair. He quoted verses from the Bible that he thought would console her, but he seemed to be unable to ease her distress. Then he suggested that she could do nothing better than to take all of her sorrow to Jesus. "You must tell Jesus," he told her. A light broke across her face and she cried, "Yes! I must tell Jesus." So she did. After a period of prayer, she rose from her knees, a new person. Mr. Hoffman left immediately with those words ringing in his ears. "I must tell Jesus." He went directly home with this inspiration and wrote:

> I must tell Jesus all of my trials;
> I cannot bear these burdens alone
> In my distress He kindly will help me;
> He ever loves and cares for His own.

> Tempted and tried, I need a great Savior,
> One who can help my burdens to bear;
> I must tell Jesus, I must tell Jesus;
> He all my cares and sorrows will share.

> Chorus:
> I must tell Jesus! I must tell Jesus!
> I cannot bear my burdens alone;
> I must tell Jesus! I must tell Jesus!
> Jesus can help me, Jesus alone.

Few gospel songs have been so dear to me. The tune carries the verses so well.

"Down at the Cross Where my Savior Died" and "Are You Washed in the Blood?" are two other favorite songs written by Elisha Hoffman that have "echoed across America for half a century."

**REFLECTION**: Sometimes we forget that God wants to help us even more than we want to help ourselves. He wants to be our friend—not a buddy or a pal, but a true friend. Remember, He sat where we sit. He was tempted in all points like as we are.

# 38

## A GREAT SOURCE OF INSPIRATION

**SCRIPTURE: John 20:1-18**

*Jesus saith unto her, Mary. She turned herself, and saith unto him, Rabboni; which is to say, Master.*

"He looked a little like a southern colonel with his white mustache and always appeared at the office with a small flower in his lapel. He had a marvelous sense of humor and a dry wit which could be very caustic if he thought the occasion demanded it—a truly brilliant man. . . ." This is a description of the late C. Austin Miles, given to me by Mrs. H. A. Dye, a friend of Mr. Miles.

His hymn "In The Garden" has become the second most popular gospel song in the United States, according to various polls. More than a million recordings of it have been sold.

One day in March, 1912, Mr. Miles was studying the twentieth chapter of John, which records the story of Mary's coming to the garden to visit the tomb of Jesus. As she looked in, her heart sank because He wasn't there. Then as He spoke to her, she recognized Him, and her heart jumped for joy. She cried, "Rabboni!"

Mr. Miles imagined that he was present with them in the garden on that glorious occasion. He leaped from his chair, inspired to write the verses of this great song. Later that same evening he wrote the music that has accompanied it on its worldwide circulation.

Mr. Miles often remarked in his later years that he would make it through another year if he could get through the month of March. Oddly enough, he passed away on March 10, 1946, in Pitman, New Jersey. Now sing his song.

> I come to the garden alone,
> While the dew is still on the roses,
> And the voice I hear,
> Falling on my ear,
> The Son of God discloses.
>
> Chorus:
> And He walks with me, and He talks with me,
> And He tells me I am His own,
> And the joy we share as we tarry there,
> None other has ever known.

**REFLECTION**: Our joy is made perfect as we share that joy with others—the joy of knowing in a personal way the Savior spoken of in the Scripture reading for today. When one seeks his own happiness he loses real and satisfying happiness. But when he turns aside to notice the plight of others, and to help, the joy of the Savior will overtake him.

# 39

## PROMISE OF HELP

**SCRIPTURE: II Corinthians 4**

*We are troubled on every side, yet not distressed; we are perplexed, but not in despair; persecuted, but not forsaken; cast down, but not destroyed.*

P.P. Bliss was well on his way to fame equal to that enjoyed by Ira D. Sankey and Fanny Crosby combined. He not only had a golden baritone voice, but was also a prolific song writer. However, a tragic train accident took the life of this young singer on December 19, 1876, when he was only thirty-eight years of age.

Once Mr. Bliss heard Major Whittle tell of a battle waged during the Civil War. On October 4, 1864, just before Sherman began his famous march to the sea, his army lay camped in the neighborhood of Atlanta. General Hood's men very carefully gained control of the rear of Sherman's army and began to cut off supply lines, burn blockhouses, and capture small garrisons of soldiers. Then General Hood moved swiftly toward the large post at Allatoona Pass. General Corse of Illinois was stationed there with fifteen hundred men to protect the large store of rations. General Hood sent word for General Corse to surrender, but Corse refused and a terrible battle ensued. After many had fallen at their post, and a continuation of the battle seemed fatal, a Union officer caught sight of a white signal flag a great distance away, on the top of Kennesaw Mountain. The signal was answered and very shortly from mountain to mountain this signal was flashed: "HOLD THE FORT; I'M COMING. W. T. SHERMAN." The Union men held on for three more hours until Sherman's forces came up and forced the retreat of Hood's Confederate forces.

Less than twenty-four hours after hearing this story, P. P. Bliss wrote the song, the title of which is inscribed on his monument at Rome, Pennsylvania:

> Ho, my comrades see the signal
> Waving in the sky.
> Reinforcements now appearing,
> Victory is nigh.
>
> Chorus:
> Hold the fort for I am coming,
> Jesus signals still;
> Wave the answer back to heaven,
> By Thy grace we will.

**REFLECTION**: If things look dark today, then remember, Jesus knows of your battle and He will come to your aid. Count it a blessing that you are in a position to rely only on Him. Stay in the fight and look for His deliverance.

If things are going well with you, look for someone else who is in need of your help. Go to his aid in Jesus' name.